iScience

Pebbles, Sand, and Silt:
The Neighbor's Garden

by Emily Sohn and Diane Bair

Chief Content Consultant
Edward Rock
Associate Executive Director, National Science Teachers Association

NORWOOD HOUSE PRESS
Chicago, IL

Norwood House Press
PO Box 316598
Chicago, IL 60631

For information regarding Norwood House Press, please visit our website at
www.norwoodhousepress.com or call 866-565-2900.

Special thanks to: Amanda Jones, Amy Karasick, Alanna Mertens, Terrence Young, Jr.

Editors: Jessica McCulloch, Barbara Foster, and Diane Hinckley
Designer: Daniel M. Greene
Production Management: Victory Productions

Library of Congress Cataloging-in-Publication Data

Sohn, Emily.

    Pebbles, sand, and silt : the neighbor's garden / by Emily Sohn and Diane Bair ;
    chief content consultant, Edward Rock.
    p. cm.—(iScience readers)

    Summary: "Describes the different kinds of soil—what makes them up and
    when to use certain soils for certain plants. As readers use scientific inquiry
    to investigate the positives and negatives of different soils, an activity based
    on real world situations challenges them to apply what they've learned in
    order to solve a puzzle"—Provided by publisher.

Includes bibliographical references and indexes.

ISBN-13: 978-1-59953-409-1 (library edition: alk. paper)
ISBN-10: 1-59953-409-6 (library edition: alk. paper)

1. Soils—Juvenile literature. I. Bair, Diane. II. Rock, Edward.

S591.3.P43 2012
631.4—dc22
2011011458

Manufactured in the United States of America in North Mankato, Minnesota.

175N—072011

Contents

Note to Caregivers:

Throughout this book, many questions are posed to the reader. Some are open-ended and ask what the reader thinks. Discuss these questions with your child and guide him or her in thinking through the possible answers and outcomes. There are also questions posed which have a specific answer. Encourage your child to read through the text to determine the correct answer. Most importantly, encourage answers grounded in reality while also allowing imaginations to soar. Information to help support you as you share the book with your child is provided in the back in the **Additional Notes** section.

Words that are **bolded** are defined in the glossary in the back of the book.

Let Your Garden Grow

Have you ever stopped to smell a flower? A healthy flower usually looks and smells beautiful. Plants, such as flowers, need the right kind of **soil** to be healthy. This book will get you digging in the ground. You will learn about soil. And you will learn the best soil to use to grow a perfect garden.

Sprouting Sunflowers

You are a gardener. An elderly neighbor has hired you. He wants you to plant a garden. He loves sunflowers. But he can't do the work himself anymore.

In his garden, you find three piles of soil.

Soil 1: This soil is mostly small rocks.

Soil 2: This soil is sandy and dry.

Soil 3: This soil is damp and dark.

You want to grow big, healthy sunflower plants. Which soil would work best?

Discover Activity

Studying Soil

You can use water to learn about soil.

1. Go out to a yard or schoolyard.
2. Use a small shovel or spoon to dig a few scoops of soil.

After step 5 your jar should look something like this one.

3. Put the soil in the jar. The jar should be one-quarter full of soil.
4. Add water until the jar is two-thirds full.
5. Put the lid on the jar.

6. Now, shake it up!

7. Wait for 30 minutes.

8. Now look at your jar.

After step 6 your jar should look something like this one.

What is at the bottom? What is near the top?

Look closely at the level of water in the jar now. How does it compare to the amount you put in? How much water do you think the soil soaked up?

The Top Layer

Stand up. Now, look down. You might be on a floor or a sidewalk. But somewhere below you, there is soil.

Some animals live in it. Plants grow in it. Soil is full of life!

What can you find in this soil?

Soil may contain bits of broken rock. There are also dead leaves in it.

What else might you find in soil? Look at the picture for ideas.

pebbles and some larger stones

Pebbles, or small, smooth rocks, are common in some soil.

These bits of rock take up space. But they don't offer food for plants.

Are there pebbles in your jar?

Would pebbles be good to have in your sunflower garden? Why or why not?

What happens when you pour water on sand?

All soils are different. Some contain **sand.**

Sand is full of **minerals** that are good for plants.

But sand is **coarse.** So it doesn't hold water very well.

Sunflowers need water.

Some soil contains **silt.**

Silt is made of tiny bits of rock. These bits are much smaller than pebbles. They are even smaller than pieces of sand.

The soil around a riverbed is often silty.

Silt offers **nutrients** to plants. It also holds water for them.

Many plants grow well in silt. But too much silt can drown plants in water.

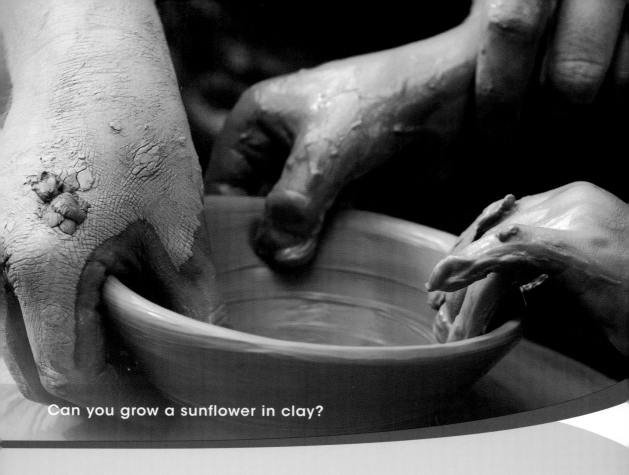

Can you grow a sunflower in clay?

Some soil contains **clay.** You may have worked with clay. It is sticky when wet.

Clay can hold food for plants. But it doesn't let much air or water in. Plants need both.

Do you want clay in your garden?

Do you think this soil would hold water well?

Each plant has its own needs. Some need more water than others. Some need loose soil.

But **humus** helps many plants grow well.

Humus contains old, dead bits of plants and animals. It is loose and spongy. It makes soil look dark.

Why might humus be good for your garden?

14

This chart shows what soil is made of. Plants get some things they need from **organic matter.** This is made of parts of dead animals and plants. They also get nutrients from **inorganic** substances, such as lime, in mineral matter.

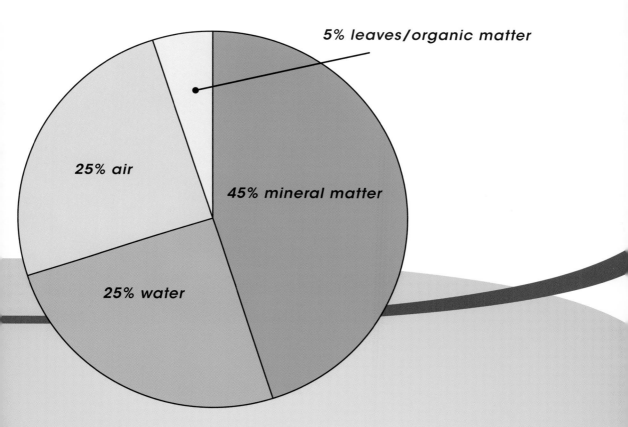

5% leaves/organic matter

25% air

45% mineral matter

25% water

Plants need water, air, and food to grow.

Good soil helps the plants get all of these.

Some soils hold more water. Other soils hold more air. Food supplies can go up and down.

Groundhogs live in tunnels underground. They sleep in the tunnels all winter.

Did You Know?

Ants, earthworms, and some snakes live in soil. So do some spiders, groundhogs, snails, and slugs.

Some creatures that live in soil are tiny. You have to use a special tool to see them. A microscope or magnifying lens would work for this.

What lives in the soil where you live? How could you find out?

Gardener

Gardeners grow plants. They might start by stirring up the soil. This way, air can get in the dirt.

Then, they put seeds in the ground. They might add nutrients or water. And they keep the weeds and pests out.

Gardening is hard work. The payoff is beauty to see and food to eat.

It feels great to eat vegetables you have grown yourself and pick your own flowers!

Worms help plants get what they need from soil.

Connecting to History

Traveling Earthworms

Earthworms look slimy. But they can help a garden.

Worms make soil looser as they crawl through the soil. This lets air and water get into the soil.

Worms also chew up dead leaves. Then they release nutrients as waste. These nutrients help plants grow.

Earthworms have not always lived in the United States. They took a long trip here. They first came with people from Europe. That was nearly 400 years ago.

The Importance of Soil

Good soil helps this farmer's crops grow. What kinds of plants do you like eating?

Plants make Earth look green and pretty. Animals eat them. And so do we. Many plants need soil to grow in. Some can grow on rocks or on other plants.

Some kinds of plants grow only in some parts of the world. Why do you think that is?

Which soil will you choose for your neighbor's garden?

Soil 1: This soil has lots of pebbles in it. It does not have many nutrients. It does not hold water very well.

Soil 2: This soil is sandy and dry. An expert could turn it into rich soil. But as it is, sunflowers will not grow well here.

Soil 3: This soil is damp and dark. It is full of water. It is also full of humus. This one is best for growing sunflowers.

Gardeners often mix soil types, too. They want plants to grow as well as they can.

These sunflowers seem to be getting what they need from the soil!

Beyond the Puzzle

Use what you have learned about soil!

Collect some soil. Put your hands in it. How can you describe it?

Is it dark or light? Is it soft or hard? Are there worms in it?

What happens if you add water? Now, put it in sunlight. How does it change?

Try to start your own garden.

Get some sunflower seeds. Put them in the soil. What do you need to do to help them grow?

What else could you grow in your garden? With the right soil, you could have the best garden in the neighborhood!

Glossary

clay: fine-grained moist dirt.

coarse: having a rough texture.

humus: organic matter from plant or animal remains.

inorganic: describes something that is not made up of living things, such as a rock.

matter: the material that things are made of.

minerals: natural substances found in Earth.

nutrients: things plants and animals need for life.

organic: describes something that is made up of living or once living things, such as leaf litter.

pebbles: small, smooth stones.

sand: loose, gritty bits of worn or broken rock.

silt: a material made of fine mineral bits smaller than in sand and larger than in clay.

soil: top layer of our planet, formed from rocks and decaying plants and animals.

Further Reading

The Dirt on Dirt, by Paulette Bourgeois. Children Can Press, 2008.

I Love Dirt! by Jennifer Ward. Trumpeter Books, 2008.

A Kid's Guide to Container Gardening, by Stephanie Bearce. Mitchell Lane, 2009.

The Dirt on Soil: What's Really Going on Under the Ground.
http://school.discoveryeducation.com/schooladventures/soil/

NASA Soil Science Education. http://soil.gsfc.nasa.gov/

Additional Notes

The page references below provide answers to questions asked throughout the book. Questions whose answers will vary are not addressed.

Page 8: Depending on the soil, there will be pebbles at the bottom, then sand, then silt. The clay will mostly stay floating in the water.

Page 9: You might find roots, ants, earthworms, or rocks in soil.

Page 10: You wouldn't want too many pebbles in your sunflower garden because there would not be enough food for the plants and water would drain right through.

Page 11: Caption question: The water runs right through the sand.

Page 13: While you wouldn't want your soil to be made up of all clay, some clay is good for retaining nutrients.

Page 14: Humus adds nutrients to the soil. Humus also helps soil retain moisture.

Index